Leo

I0893319

22 July – 22 August

amber
BOOKS

ASTROLOGICAL SIGN DATES:
The precise start and end times for each sign vary by a day or two from year to year as the Gregorian calendar shifts relative to the tropical year. The dates provided in this book are correct for the year 2020.

If you are unsure of the Zodiac sign for your specific birth year, visit: www.yourzodiacsign.com.

Leo

22 July – 22 August

A guide to understanding yourself, your friendships and finding your true love

This edition first published in 2020 by
Amber Books Ltd
United House
North Road
London N7 9DP
United Kingdom
www.amberbooks.co.uk
Instagram: amberbooksltd
Facebook: amberbooks
Twitter: @amberbooks

Copyright © 2020 Amber Books Ltd

All rights reserved. No part of this work may be reproduced, stored in a retrieval system, or transmitted in any form or by any means, electronic, mechanical, photocopying, recording, or otherwise, without the prior permission of the copyright holder.

ISBN: 978-1-83886-025-7

Project Editor: Sarah Uttridge
Design: Zoë Mellors

Picture Credits:
All illustrations by Fabbri Publications except the following:
Shutterstock: 31 (Elena Naumchenkova), 32 (La Puma), 35 (Slonomysh)

Printed and bound in China

TRADITIONAL CHINESE BOOKBINDING

This book has been produced using traditional Chinese bookbinding techniques, using a method that was developed during the Ming Dynasty (1368–1644) and remained in use until the adoption of Western binding techniques in the early 1900s. In traditional Chinese binding, single sheets of paper are printed on one side only, and each sheet is folded in half, with the printed pages on the outside. The book block is then sandwiched between two boards and sewn together through punched holes close to the cut edges of the folded sheets.

Contents

Introduction

Leo

22 July–22 August

Sign: The Lion

Ruling Planet: The Sun

Gender: Masculine

Element: Fire

Quality: Fixed

Compatibility: Cancer, Aquarius and Virgo

Non-compatibility: Scorpio and Gemini

Every man, woman and child is born with a distinct and different destiny. There are no exceptions. Everyone has cosmic significance and a part to play in the life of the universe. This is innate and inescapable, and goes beyond the tiny boundaries of nation, creed and colour.

As we live out our lives on planet Earth, we are, however unknowingly, acting in a greater drama and reacting to impulses that come from distant astronomical bodies, stars and planets millions of light years away. Sceptics pour scorn on the idea that far-distant Saturn, for example, can have any effect on our lives, as the ancient art and science of astrology teaches. But the fact is that we are sparks of energy inhabiting bodies made of the same stuff as the stars, responding like tiny radios to the distant messages they send to Earth.

Each infant carries within it a double blueprint for life: its genetic programming and the pattern of character that comes from the astrological 'clock' that was set in motion at the moment of birth. No one knows the full extent of genetic influence, although it seems to be astonishingly far-reaching, but the power of the horoscope has been well known to the wisest men and women for many centuries.

Our Sun and Moon signs provide essential inside information about our destinies. They reveal the secrets of who we really are, and why we are here, laying out before us our potential, the sort of joys and achievements our characteristics may bring about, and warn us of problems to be overcome through the triumph of free will.

Read this book with an open mind and discover who you really are.

The Elements

Up to the beginning of the Age of Enlightenment – the modern scientific era – in the 18th century, it was commonly believed that everything, including human beings, was made up of the four elements: Earth, Air, Fire and Water. These were thought of as the building blocks of life, and each astrological sign had a predominance of one or another. Each created its common characteristics, although too much of any of the elements can produce an unbalanced personality.

Fire Signs

The Fire signs are Aries, Leo and Sagittarius. Consumed with passion – which all too often, however, takes the form of self-love and burning ambition – these are the natural stars of the zodiac. They are fired up with motivation, and sparks really fly when they get going. It is difficult to keep a Fire sign doing things at a measured pace (steady old Taureans can sometimes do it, though) because their enthusiasms soon spread like wildfire, catching the imaginations of more and more people. Fire signs are the leaders – especially Leo, King of the Jungle, which is the most regal and imperious of all the signs of the zodiac.

They do, nevertheless, have great warmth and charisma, and light the way for others to follow. Arians can burn with a cold flame or with the raging fires of revolution. Either way, their passion is based on a childlike – even childish – desire to get their own way, without any thought for the future or the feelings of others. But they are willing to go where others fear to tread, and without them human progress would always be a great deal slower and more difficult.

Sagittarians are the great enthusiasts of the zodiac, sparky and constantly generating yet more energy. Like the centaur-archer and the horse-man of their sign, Sagittarians can rush into things, galloping at the gate that is never going to open magically at the last minute, or shooting very wide of the mark. But they will pick themselves up and start again, uncomplainingly, forever encouraging more timid souls, and all while keeping their own eyes on new horizons.

Fire Signs

Aries

Leo

Sagittarius

Colours of the Zodiac

Traditionally, each sign of the zodiac has its own colour, which is believed to be 'lucky' or magically empowered for those born under that particular sign. In general, the colours are associated with the ruling planets and are symbolic of their attributes. Many people find that they feel most comfortable when wearing their sign's colours, and often choose them without knowing their full astrological background.

Leo

Ruling Planet: The Sun

Colours: Gold, yellowy-orange and sometimes red. These are the colours of ambition and extroverts, of bold Leos who seek the limelight. More timid people can benefit from wearing them, but naturally strong personalities may need to tone them down.

The Angelic Hierarchy

According to ancient tradition, each planet is governed by one of the great archangels, who are also rulers of certain aspects of human life. The box below lists the planet that they rule, the areas over which they have influence and their special day of the week.

Michael

Archangel of the Sun.

Governs: Leo.

Rules: Human destiny, ambition, monetary gain, careers and motivation.

Day: Sunday.

The Genders

Traditionally, the twelve signs of the zodiac are divided into Masculine and Feminine, although of course both men and women are born into each.

The characteristics were assigned to the genders aeons ago, well before modern feminism or political correctness, and may now seem old-fashioned to many. However, the signs do seem to be grouped according to the appropriate gender.

The Masculine Signs

The Masculine signs are Aries, Gemini, Leo, Libra, Sagittarius and Aquarius. Masculine traits do tend to be accentuated in the Fire signs, which are Aries, Leo and Sagittarius.

Masculine signs are dominant and assertive, often to the point of being pugnacious and extroverted. They are natural leaders and rulers, showing fiery initiative, and are fiercely protective of others in their care. They are pioneers and visionaries, conquerors of new lands and the first to achieve great things. They tend to tackle things themselves and can be impatient with others who are less assertive.

Negatively, Masculine signs can be egotistical, arrogant and cruel, and dismissive of the needs and feelings of others. They can also tend to be trouble-makers and rebels – violent, belligerent and inclined to subversion.

The Ruling Planets

Until the 18th century, astrologers knew only the planets of our solar system that could be seen with the naked eye: Mercury, Venus, Mars, Jupiter and Saturn. (For the purposes of astrology, the Sun and the Moon are also counted as planets, even though the Sun is a star and the Moon is the satellite of Earth.) Uranus was discovered in 1781, Neptune in 1846 and Pluto was first seen in 1930. Many astrologers believe that the existence of other heavenly bodies – such as the rumoured Vulcan, which hypothetically exists within the orbit of Mercury – is about to be confirmed. Astrologers will then have to agree which signs these 'new' planets will rule, and what human characteristics their discovery will accentuate.

The Sun

Many ancient civilizations worshipped the Sun, seeing in its brightness the potential perfection of humanity. Zeus, Helios, Mithras, Ra, Atum and Aten were just some of the many Sun gods who were venerated millennia ago. Lucifer, now seen as synonymous with Satan in the West, was originally a beneficent Sun-god. His name simply means 'light-bringer', or illuminator of the spirit. The goddess Diana was known as 'Diana Lucifera', and Mary Magdalene was also called 'Mary Lucifera' by the early Gnostic Church, in honour of their power to illuminate the souls of men. It seems that Luciferans were not the evil Satanists of popular imagination, but were in reality adherents of a Gnostic belief system that celebrated personal knowledge of,

About the Sun

The Sun, around which nine planets and their satellites revolve, is the life-giver of our solar system. Without it, everything would die. It is about 150 million km (93 million miles) from Earth and is so large that approximately 110 Earths could be fitted inside it.

The day that was originally sacred to the Sun was, of course, Sunday.

and enlightenment by, the light of God. Gold and kingship are associated with the Sun, the ruler of Leo and archetypical sign of royalty, nobility and worldly achievement. Its fire inspires loyalty, joie de vivre and ambition. However, Sun subjects can be ruthless, patronizing and overbearing, and their fire can die very quickly, leaving them lazy and downcast.

The Qualities

In addition to the influence of gender, the elements and the planets, each sign of the zodiac is affected by having an intrinsic quality – Cardinal, Fixed or Mutable.

Cardinal Quality

Those with a strong Cardinal quality to their chart are, traditionally, supremely ambitious and perhaps somewhat ruthless in getting to the top. They are bursting with ideas and are dynamic in pursuing their goals, especially where their careers are concerned. They see themselves as achievers and winners: every day is a challenge that they willingly accept. Their sense of determination inspires others, although they themselves will continue to take the lead and initiate every new project. They can be dismissive of lesser mortals. Cardinality also represents new beginnings.

Leo

Those born under the sign of the Lion believe that they have a natural nobility and that they are leaders. Their innate laziness, however, makes them disinclined to stir from any comfortable situation, be it a job, a life partnership or a particular house. They hate change for its own sake and, despite their ambition, they lack the necessary stamina to fight their rivals to the bitter end.

Signs and Symbols

Most people are familiar with the zodiac 'zoo' – the collection of symbols that represent the twelve signs. These images reflect the characteristics traditionally assigned to each sign and contain a wealth of knowledge about its true nature.

Each sign of the zodiac is represented by a symbol – the twin fish for Pisces, for example. No one is sure exactly when or why the symbols were chosen, although some authorities believe they date from Sumeria or Mesopotamia, 4000 years before Jesus Christ. The priest-astrologers of the ancient world were the first to impose recognizable patterns on the great constellations – Leo the Lion being one example.

Today, seeing such shapes in the stars may seem fanciful, but thousands of years ago imaginations were more poetic, and many myths told of magical animals, such as the dragon, which had strange powers to influence everyday human life.

Although the ancient Egyptians left few astrological records, they were almost unique in antiquity for worshipping archetypal, animal-headed gods. However, these strange hybrid gods – half-human, half-animal – were worshipped as aspects of one God. Contrary to the general belief that the Egyptians were idolaters, their religion was basically monotheistic. Each statue represented an aspect of the one true God.

Since they were established, the signs have remained unchanged, although there was a movement in the Middle Ages to change the sign of Aquarius into the sign of John the Baptist – presumably because of the connection with water.

The twelve signs of the zodiac do seem particularly apt on the whole, and accurately reflect the archetypal character of Sun sign types. The great Swiss psychoanalyst Carl Gustav Jung (1875–1961) believed that, deep in our psyches, humanity shares a collective unconscious – a set of archetypal images, which, at a profound level, we all understand. The signs of the zodiac form part of this pool of images, conveying eternal truths to our unconscious minds.

Signs and Symbols

Aries

Taurus

Gemini

Cancer

Leo

Virgo

Libra

Scorpio

Sagittarius

Capricorn

Aquarius

Pisces

Leo The Lion

Lions are magnificent beasts – strong, athletic and noble. They can be excellent hunters, although it is the lionesses who usually do the lion's share of the work. Sometimes, even the king of the jungle stoops to stealing the kills of others. They are good protectors of their pride but can be irascible, chasing off those who challenge their male supremacy. They can even kill their own offspring should they have the temerity to be demanding or too playful.

Throughout history, because lions have always represented kingship, ferocious strength and nobility, their image has often been incorporated into heraldic devices such as banners or shields. The archetypal appeal of the beast can be seen in the adoption of powerful names such as 'Lionheart' for King Richard I of England and 'The Lion of Judah' for the emperors of Ethiopia.

In the so-called 'black art' of alchemy, which was

outlawed by the Church, the lion represented the uncontrolled forces of nature in the real world.

In ancient Egyptian mythology, Sekhmet, the lioness-headed goddess, was the avenger and protector of her worshippers. She was the daughter of the great sun god Ra, and her name meant 'powerful' or 'mightiest'. Her other titles included 'Lady of the Flame', reflecting Leo's association with fire.

The story goes that Sekhmet was instructed, in the name of her father, to punish humanity for its waywardness, but once unleashed, her vengeance far outstripped his intentions and nearly destroyed the world. The only way she could be halted was by tempting her with rivers of beer – which she drank. Afterwards, she fell asleep, fortunately forgetting to annihilate humankind. But Sekhmet had a gentler side and was very popular among those who needed courage in their endeavours.

Because she answered the prayers of a certain Pharaoh, granting him triumph in battle, he raised over four hundred statues to her in Egypt. To this day, there are more statues of Sekhmet than of any other Egyptian deity, many of which are in Western museums. She is now a great favourite with New Agers.

The Sun in Leo

Sun sign Leos are powerful, ambitious and protective – truly the kings of the jungle. Ruled by the Sun, they are outgoing and optimistic, their sunny disposition often inspiring lesser mortals to greater efforts. They are the party animals of the zodiac, dynamic and uninhibited, believing they can achieve whatever they set out to. New York is the perfect city for a Leo. As natural leaders, they love being top of the heap, their innate reserves of energy and self-belief helping them to overcome any setbacks. To Leos, integrity and dignity are as natural as breathing. Warm-hearted and often extremely generous, they love company – especially if they are the centre of attention. Their enthusiasm is contagious, especially when it comes to motivating others in more creative endeavours. Well-aspected Sun sign Leos are intrinsically faithful partners and loyal friends, and extremely loving in a very demonstrative, expansive way. When life is good for a Leo, everyone in their circle benefits in some way.

Conversely, when Leos are crossed and their integrity or self-esteem is challenged, they can fly into towering rages – which may soon evaporate, but they can leave those at the receiving end shaken to the core. It is easy for Leos to become overbearing. Sometimes they seem to demand worship from those closest to them, without realizing that respect must be earned. Some Leos are out-and-out bullies, taking advantage of any weakness in others, while many can be domineering and unapproachable, both at work and at home. They can also be extremely dogmatic and ruthless in pursuing their particular ideology, giving no thought to the differing beliefs and lifestyles of others. Weakness or illness irritates

Personality Traits of Leos

Positive	*Negative*
Ambitious	Overbearing
Powerful	Bullies
Protective	Tendency to fly into rages
Outgoing	Domineering
Optimistic	Unapproachable
Party animals	Dogmatic
Generous	Pompous
Warm-hearted	
Loyal	

this type and provokes them into unkindness, even cruelty. Even the lesser Leonine tyrants can be amazingly pompous, often speaking on a one-to-one basis as if addressing a formal meeting, and inevitably patronizing those they consider to be their inferiors. Badly aspected Leos are often misogynists or racists, in much the same way as their fellow Fire sign, Aries. However, the Lion's bigotry arises out of a basic lack of tolerance of any threat to their leadership.

Even Leos who appear to be quiet and restrained have all the virtues and flaws of the typical, expansive Lion. If you want to see Leos turn from pussycat into magnificent, terrifying king of the jungle, just injure their pride or treat them with contempt. Then the seemingly docile housecat shakes out its mane and growls ferociously.

Appearance

The major characteristic of the Leonine appearance is gloriously abundant hair, often reddish or tawny coloured; it is a true mane, wavy and untamed. Leos have 'big hair' to match their big personalities. They tend to be dramatic and prone to the occasional bad day, when nothing works out and the Sun that rules them is blotted out by a haze of gloom. Slow and deliberate in speech and movement, their bearing is regal and dignified. They tend to have a direct stare, which can be unnerving, and curiously wide or upward slanting eyes, giving them an unusual and rather theatrical appearance. Their complexion is youthful, but also somewhat sallow. When suntanned, they look far more stunning than any other sign. They dress in the best of taste, but are too impatient to drag endlessly around the shops, contenting themselves with one or two good outfits in which they know they can stop the traffic.

Health

Leos tend to suffer from heart trouble: their lion hearts take so much stress, both emotional and physical, that sooner or later they will have a health scare and become very heart-conscious, though usually late in the day. Until that

moment, however, they tend to indulge their love of high-fat luxury foods and good wines, as befits their innate regality. They also tend, for the same reasons, to put on weight, but rarely attempt to do anything about it for long, although expensive spas and intensive pampering will certainly appeal to them. They may be far too lazy to follow a regular exercise programme, but by employing personal trainers they can be weaned off the sedentary life. Anything that requires ugly sweating in a group of lesser mortals is absolute anathema to them.

Leos also suffer from back and spine problems, made worse by their tendency to be overweight and their lack of exercise. However, they can ease their discomfort by doing regular stretching exercises and visiting the chiropractor or osteopath.

Career

Leos are happiest and most effective in any career where they can give orders or be the centre of attention. Being second-in-command or a humble team member is not for them, and their irritation at working – as they see it – for and with fools will not make for a happy workplace. When a Leo is upset, everyone soon knows about it. Teaching gives them the opportunity to take charge and also to express their creativity and pass on their often considerable wisdom to the next generation. Leos are often the teachers who make a lasting impression on the children in their care. They may tend to have mood swings and can be irascible one minute, but capable of making the whole class rock with mirth at some joke or anecdote the next – all acted out with great gusto and a complete lack of inhibition. Their enthusiasms can inspire pupils for life, although they can also destroy the confidence of more timid children – such as Sun sign Cancerians – with too much over-hearty teasing and the occasional outburst of titanic temper.

Leos have a natural bent for the theatre and the performing arts. This is why they are so much at home in the acting and singing professions, and are often excellent dancers. They are never content to take just any part that comes along, but will use these more humble occupations as a means to an end – to progress to higher things. Working with these potential stars of the show is not easy. Leos can be tiresome as one of an ensemble, and constantly seek to upstage the others – even at the expense of the show as a whole or at the expense of personal feelings. Other flamboyant Leos find fulfilment in

The best careers for Leos

- Teacher
- Actor
- Singer
- Theatre manager
- Dancer
- Model
- Designer

the glamour industries of fashion, modelling and design – anything, in fact, that is luxurious and impressive and has panache.

Even Leos without that overwhelming urge to see their name in lights need to feel that what they do is of real value and that their contribution is meaningful. Despite their desire to show off, Leos are fair-minded and meticulous in keeping agreements. They expect others to be the same.

Whatever they do, they expect their attention to be fully engaged, and to be constantly praised and given positive feedback. They can't do any job for long, especially something routine or tedious, without bursting out and opting for something that offers to fulfil their considerable potential. Never take a Leo for granted, or expect them to beaver away without any recognition. Bosses with Leo employees should be particularly careful – Leo the Lion could be after their jobs.

Relationships

Leos make wonderfully sociable companions: amusing, urbane and expansive. They tend to have a large circle of friends, many of them close and many for life. If they can afford it (and often even if they can't), they will pick up the tab in restaurants or host lavish parties. Gregarious and charming, they rarely live alone, even if it means sharing their home with several cats and dogs, to whom they are devoted.

Leos are usually fairly easy to live with, although they do expect others to live up to their own high standards as they cannot tolerate failure. They often expect life partners to be almost as ambitious as themselves. Leos love luxury and the best of everything, and tend to be snobbish. Status means everything to certain extreme Leo types. Because of this, they may even choose to live in an area where they don't really feel at home simply because it is 'posh' or 'up-and-coming'. A Leo is usually nobody's fool, but they can make easy prey for astute estate agents with impressive properties for sale. They are not obsessively tidy and prefer a cosy home where they can relax and enjoy family life. Although they love the planning stages of interior design and home decorating, they are far too grand and lazy to get their own hands dirty. They are quite happy to pay for someone else to do the work.

Leos suffer from a certain dichotomy. Although they frequently lay on the charm thickly, they can be ruthless at the same time, a combination of the appealing and appalling. Male Leos can be surprisingly lazy, often giving up a project for the sake of a holiday or changing to something else quite abruptly. The lioness, however, is almost always on the alert, whether it is for the bargain of a lifetime, the dream partner or the big break that leads to success. These are qualities that can disrupt a happy home, but once they are accepted as congenital in Leos, other zodiac signs are more or less able to live with them.

Although Leos are passionate and faithful lovers, they may look elsewhere if their partners betray them or injure their over-developed sense of pride. These partners tread on dangerous ground if they laugh at an inappropriate moment, or even try to provide comfort and understanding at difficult times in a Leo's sex life – worse still, if they show Leos up in any way. Apart from failure, what Leos hate most is boredom and pessimism. Anyone gloomy and uninspired by nature will not last the course with a typical Sun sign Leo. They relish the chance to laugh and be sociable, and to wine and dine their loved ones. They enjoy lavishing romantic gifts on them. In return, they expect to be showered with compliments and praised to the heavens. Although they can often see through the more crude type of insincerity, flattery will get you almost anywhere with a Leo.

Leos can be difficult parents. They try very hard to enter into the child's world by playing rumbustious games and acting out bedtime stories at great length – and never mind if their partners are just longing for the little dears to go to sleep. It is in the nature of the Lion to want to be in control where children are concerned. This is why they are interfering, bossy and often extremely demanding. Unfortunately, the Leo parent can destroy the confidence of delicate flowers and fail to understand their more introspective children, who may be very grateful for the drama lessons and birthday parties for 200 with a famous conjuror for entertainment, but would really rather stay home and read a book.

There is often an ambivalence in Leos' attitude to successful partners, siblings or children. Leos can be very competitive, although many of them also expect to succeed without really having to fight against anything other than Fate. To take on anyone else as a competitor tends to make them quickly feel stressed and threatened.

Leos – male and female – need to be wary of feelings of jealousy creeping in when they are confronted with their children's successes. They will, however, usually take some comfort in the thought that those very successes are in some way part of their own achievement as a parent.

Ideal Partner

Leos, especially men, can make a happy lifelong commitment to the emotional and home-loving Cancerian or the supportive, stable Taurean. There will, of course, be problems, for Leos expect primacy and deference, and even the most martyrly Cancerian will sometimes feel slighted by this situation. Gentle Aquarians, who may be knowledgeable astrologers and therefore forewarned, can cope better with Leo's demands, although they may not always be there when needed. Aquarians are often too busy with good causes to provide the consistent support that Leos expect. As far as Virgoans are concerned, the straightforward and usually well-grounded Leos can be complementary partners, since Virgo is the sign of the organized. However, Leos are often attracted, sometimes with disastrous results, to the fascinating Scorpian or flighty Geminian. Generally, however, Leos are magnanimous and can be adaptable. As long as they are fully supported and loved, they can conduct a successful relationship with almost any sign.

Compatibility in Relationships

Aries
20 March–19 April

Matching fire with fire – and ego with ego – is not a good recipe for a harmonious and loving relationship.

Capricorn
21 December–20 January

Any initial attraction will soon wear thin due to the Goat's innate distrust of Leonine extravagance.

Cancer
21 June–21 July

This is an enviable partnership: more well-balanced Cancerians can make a happy nest with a beloved Leo.

Taurus
20 April–20 May

Steady, feet-on-the-ground Taureans can make it work with Leos but, too often, there will be a spark missing.

Libra
23 September–22 October

Librans and Leos are mutually attracted, but the Scales dither too much for decisive, opinionated Leo.

Leo
22 July–22 August

There can never be two kings in the same jungle. One will be forced to back off or submit. Not a happy pairing.

Scorpio
23 October–21 November

There will be great sex and memorable times, but the intensity will cause too many problems in the long term.

Virgo
23 August–22 September

More relaxed Virgoans can hit it off fairly well with expansive Leos, but most are too inhibited to try.

Aquarius
21 January–18 February

Leos can make a go of it with big-thinking Aquarians, but they may need more support than is forthcoming.

Sagittarius
22 November–20 December

All fire and energy, these two will wear each other out with their headlong rush at life and fierce power struggles.

Gemini
21 May–20 June

Good times will be enjoyed, but difficult-to-pin-down Geminians will not provide Leo with the right home life.

Pisces
19 February–19 March

This combination makes for a roller-coaster partnership. The water, in this case, is more likely to put out the fire.

The Leo Child

Leo children are assertive, organized and enthusiastic, and are often independent from an early age. They are able to charm adults with their bright intellects and sunny temperaments. As long as they are given due recognition that their place in the pecking order is at the top, Leos are relatively problem-free as children. However, if their leadership is questioned or others fail to fall in with their way of doing things, they can be extremely bossy and aggressive, hitting out both physically and verbally.

Although, at heart, Leos want to be liked, what they really crave is the near adulation of siblings, schoolfriends, parents and teachers. This they see as their unalienable right, whether or not they have earned it. Fortunately, this tendency can be positively sublimated by solo sports or the starring role in the school play, or simply by being given greater responsibility and a good 'talking to' that appeals to the Leo sense of pride and honour. Most Leos, however, are naturally good citizens and may eventually seek prominent roles on their local council or become leading lights in Parent–Teacher Associations.

If by any chance praise and encouragement are not forthcoming, Leo children may just give up. Their natural indolence persuades them that the fight isn't worth the trouble. Often their achievements are in direct proportion to the high or low expectations of their teachers or their parents.

If their life is hard, deprived of treats, holidays and luxuries, Leos will feel diminished as people and personally insulted by Fate. Though little demoralizes the sunny Leo for very long, they find physical or financial hardship difficult to bear, and need extra love and support from their parents in such adverse circumstances. What gets them through is a dream, something to aim for, the light at the end of the tunnel. Many Leos succeed in life against all odds, simply because their nature demands that they must win or die.

Famous Leos

Queen Elizabeth the Queen Mother

Napoleon Bonaparte

Robert Mitchum

Madonna

Robert Redford

Fidel Castro

Leonard Bernstein

Emily Brontë

Coco Chanel

Claude Debussy

Cecil B. DeMille

Robert de Niro

Mick Jagger

George Bernard Shaw

Benito Mussolini

Percy Bysshe Shelley

Sir Alexander Fleming

Dustin Hoffman

Carl G. Jung

Guy de Maupassant

Finding Your Sun Sign (2020 dates)

Aries	20 March–19 April*
Taurus	20 April–20 May
Gemini	21 May–20 June
Cancer	21 June–21 July
Leo	22 July–22 August
Virgo	23 August–22 September
Libra	23 September–22 October
Scorpio	23 October–21 November
Sagittarius	22 November–20 December
Capricorn	21 December–20 January
Aquarius	21 January–18 February
Pisces	19 February–19 March

*The dates provided in this book reflect the year 2020.
Dates may vary by a day or two from year to year.